Holida
from Nature

CONTENTS

Introduction

For years, I shopped for Christmas and Hanukkah gifts in the conventional way — going to crowded malls, waiting in long lines, spending too much money, and emerging with gifts that were "good enough" but seemed to be missing something.

Then it occurred to me to combine my lifelong interest in crafts such as wreath making with my desire to give more unique and personal holiday gifts. Creating gifts from nature is infinitely more pleasurable than shopping in stores, and it saves money. Equally important, making your own gifts saves time. You can work on gift projects at the time of year that suits your own schedule best, organizing your work in stages or doing it all in larger blocks of time.

After reading this booklet, you will be able to create the projects described here as well as use your imagination to improvise on variations. The step-by-step instructions are simple and basic, suitable for both the novice and the experienced crafter. In some cases, packaging ideas are also suggested, but for many of these projects, the gift in itself is already a beautiful presentation.

Wreaths

As one of the oldest holiday traditions, wreaths have become ubiquitous in December. In certain parts of the country, it has even become customary to keep them up until spring as a way to brighten the long winter months. Wreaths make wonderful holiday gifts, not only as seasonal decorations for doors, mantelpieces, or centerpieces, but also — in herbal versions — for year-round decorating anywhere in the home.

Best of all, wreaths are easy and inexpensive to make. When you're ready to present your handmade wreath, simply add a hand-printed tag that lists the ingredients or contains a holiday wish.

QUICKIE SPICE WREATH

adapted from *Herbs for Weddings & Other Celebrations*

These adorable aromatic wreaths can be created in miniature to use as favors or made large to serve as decorations. For a variation, apply the project steps below to a Styrofoam ball and present it as a topiary decoration. Once all the ingredients below are assembled, you'll be ready to make many spicy wreaths. Why not organize a workshop?

What You Will Need

Styrofoam rings
Brown florist's tape or textured fabric
Hanger
Glue
Assortment of dried materials from herb garden
**   or spice cupboard**

1. Use Styrofoam ring of desired size purchased at any craft shop or cut from cardboard, and wrap with brown florist's tape or textured fabric.

2. Attach a small hanger at the back.

3. Cover the wreath generously with glue. Embed bay leaves; small nuts, pinecones, or acorns; bits of cinnamon bark; vanilla beans; whole aniseed, dill, cumin, caraway, poppyseeds — anything dried from your herb garden or spice cupboard. Whole cloves and star anise are both especially fragrant and attractive. For color, glue on cardamom, dried orange peel, petals, rose hips, candied ginger, pistachios, whatever is available. Look around you, especially on the spice shelf in your favorite store, with an eye toward color, size, shape, and texture as well as fragrance.

4. Allow your wreath to dry thoroughly.

5. Fasten on a bow, if you wish.

For an aromatic miniature wreath, attach a variety of dried pods and spices to a small wreath form.

HANDMADE HOLIDAY WREATH

adapted from *Christmas Trees*

Single-faced wreaths, made by wiring the greens on only one side of a wreath ring, are designed for hanging on a wall or door or to use as a centerpiece. Double-faced wreaths, with greens on both sides of the ring, are preferred by most people because they are more bushy and, since the wreath wire is hidden, they can be hung in windows.

What You Will Need
Tips of seasonal greens such as fir, holly, boxwood,
    pine or spruce
Hand pruners
Crimped wreath ring of desired size
23-guage wire

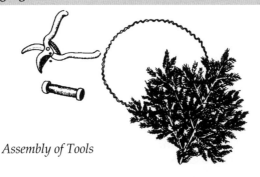

Assembly of Tools

1. Wind a few twists of wire around the wreath ring to fasten it securely.

2. Place a bunch of two to four tips of greens on one side of the ring. Wire the base of the bunch to the ring with two or three tight wraps around. Select some good bushy greens for this first bunch, because it must hide the base of the last bunch you'll insert. If you are making a double-faced wreath, flip the ring over, and use the same method to wrap a similar bunch onto the back side. Place it almost, but not quite, opposite the first one.

3. Lay another bunch of greens over the base of the first bunch, hiding the wire, and wire this one to the ring. Continue in this fashion all the way around the ring. If it is a double-faced wreath, continue wiring on both sides, gently turning the ring over after each bunch is secured.

Securing greens to the ring

4. When you reach the spot where you began, tuck the base of the last bunch underneath the tops of the first that you wired. Wire it in carefully, so neither the stems nor the wire show.

5. Cut or break the wire and fasten it tightly with several twists to one of the wires or to the ring itself.

Wreath-Making Tip

Since the upper and lower sides of greens such as fir, holly, and boxwood look quite different, they must be "faced" when placing them on the ring so the pale side won't show. Pines look the same on both sides, so this facing is not necessary.

Herbal Creations

The eloquence of herbs is never more apparent than at holiday time. They speak of many things — of ancient wisdom and future joy. Gifts made from herbs are not only a pleasure to give, they are equally delightful to make! You can use fresh, dried, or pressed herbs in any quantity available to you. Pick and choose from the projects below gifts that suit each person's lifestyle best, and build upon the suggestions with your own improvisations.

HERB BOUQUET

adapted from *Herbs for Weddings & Other Celebrations*

Basic flower arranging is a breeze if you follow the principles outlined below. Vertical, horizontal, or triangular designs are traditional and easiest to accomplish, and they usually work well for herbal arrangements, whether large or small. Choose a beautiful vase and plan your arrangement with its size in mind, deciding in advance how tall and how wide the arrangement should be.

What You Will Need
Vase in desired shape, color, and size
Herbs, foliage, and flowers of varying lengths, the longest being twice the height of the vase

---

1. Position the tallest and longest side stems of your herbs, foliage, or flowers first. Use a ruler if you need to. This is the skeleton of your arrangement; never extend outside this framework.

2. Fill in these outermost perimeters with slightly shorter materials, both herbs and foliage, fleshing out your pattern.

3. Tuck more herbs and greens in between. I call this the "poke and shove" method of flower arranging. Don't be timid. Although your bouquet may look sparse and funny at first, poke and shove to your heart's content. Be assured it will work.

4. Fill in from behind as well as in front, angling materials as necessary to conform to your original basic pattern. Stems of varying lengths will give the proper fullness, depth, and dimension. The arrangement should not have the uniform appearance of a clipped hedge.

5. Finally, place your flowers strategically here and there, angling them so that all their faces are visible from all perspectives. If you have enough flowers, tuck a few in the back to complete your arrangement properly.

6. Add decorative elements such as baby's breath or bows last, if desired.

7. Mist thoroughly, swathe in sheets of plastic, and keep shaded and cool until time to present your beautiful fragrant bouquet.

Create oversize bouquets in large vases.

POTPOURRI PARASOL

adapted from *Herbs for Weddings & Other Celebrations*

This unique fragrance packet makes a welcome gift for anyone who likes pretty things. It is surprisingly easy and inexpensive to create. Why not make several?

What You Will Need

2 pieces of calico fabric (in holiday colors if desired), 10"x10"
One 8-inch and one 22-inch length of ½-inch lace and
** coordinating thread**
One 12-inch pipe cleaner
¼ cup fragrant potpourri
One narrow satin ribbon (12 inches long)

1. Enlarge the parasol pattern shown on page 9 and use it to cut two pieces from the calico. The long sides of each piece should measure approximately 9 inches.

2. With the wrong sides of the calico together, stitch the sides together, taking ¼-inch seams. Turn right side out, and press with a warm iron.

3. Hand sew or machine stitch the 22-inch length of lace around the top edge of the parasol pouch so that the lace ruffles rise upward. Hand stitch the 8-inch length of lace around the bottom edge, lace ruffles downward. Be careful not to stitch across the bottom opening of the pouch.

4. Insert the pipe cleaner down the middle of the parasol. Position it so that approximately 2 to 3 inches show at the bottom. Stitch in place across the bottom.

5. Gather the bottom of the parasol with basting stitches and pull it closed. Secure the pouch with tiny stitches.

Potpourri-filled parasols make thoughtful holiday gifts.

6. Stuff the parasol with your favorite potpourri (see below for the recipes).

7. Baste around the top and gather to close. Hand stitch the top closure carefully, securing with tiny stitches. Tie the narrow satin ribbon in place just below the lace edge, and make a bow.

8. Bend the upper portion of the pipe cleaner to form the handle.

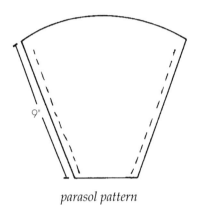

parasol pattern

Recipes for Potpourri

Rose Jar Potpourri

Rose petals, dried
¼ cup Kosher salt
¼ ounce each ground cloves, mace, and allspice
½ ounce ground cinnamon
¼ pound lavender flowers
¼ ounce toilet water or cologne (preferably lavender)
A few drops of rose oil
2 ounces of orrisroot

Mixed Bag Potpourri

1 quart dried herbs and flowers
½ cup patchouli
¼ cup sandlewood chips
¼ cup vetiver roots
1 teaspoon each frankincense, myrrh, ground cloves, and ground cinnamon
1 tonka bean, finely chopped
¼ cup ground allspice
10 drops rose oil
1 cup ground orrisroot

Carefully and gently mix together the ingredients of your potpourri. Store in a tightly closed container for 3–4 weeks until well blended.

SOFT SCULPTURE

adapted from *Herbs for Weddings & Other Celebrations*

This fabric-enshrouded pot of herbs makes an entertaining gift or centerpiece. Once you see how beautiful your creation is, you'll want to make many of them.

What You Will Need

Pot of herbs
Plastic or foil
Batting or tissue paper
Square of calico or holiday fabric large enough to cover pot
Ribbon or yarn long enough to tie around pot rim

1. Cover the pots with plastic or foil, so they may be watered easily and kept alive.

2. Wrap each pot with batting or tissue to give it some puffiness. Set the pot on the square of fabric. (See illustration A.)

3. Gather the fabric up around the rim and tie it with contrasting ribbons or wool yarn. (See illustration B.)

A

Place pot, foil, and batting on colorful fabric.

B

Bundle fabric around rim of pot and tie off with a ribbon.

Nature Prints

Simple nature prints make beautiful gifts that can be worn, framed, or displayed. This centuries-old process of recreating images from the natural world requires only a natural object, pigment, and a printable surface such as paper or fabric. It is a low-cost process that yields unlimited possibilities, restricted only by your imagination and the natural objects available to you. Described below are two of my favorite nature printing projects for holiday giving.

LEAF-STAMPED STATIONERY

adapted from *Nature Printing with Herbs, Fruits & Flowers*

Leaf stamping is an easy way to create beautiful gift packets of stationery for letters, memos, postcards, and envelopes. The design possibilities are endless for place cards, note cards, holiday cards, labels, and gift wrap as well. Almost anyone will appreciate a gift of hand-printed stationery, whether they use it for handwritten letters or computer-printed and faxed messages.

Leaf stamps can be used to ornament stationery, cards, envelopes, labels and invitations.

Heather Windfield
13 Sage Lane
Hawthorne Hill, VT

What You Will Need

Stamp pads (colors of your choice)
Tweezers
Variety of small leaves
Typing paper, copier paper, or stationery of your choice
Envelopes to fit selected paper

1. Using a stamp pad and tweezers, ink several small leaves on both sides. Turn over each leaf once or twice while pressing it on the stamp pad to ensure enough ink has adhered. (*Note:* Stamp pad embossing inks and powders create glossy, raised designs that look very professional. However, some printers and fax machines may not accept paper with glossy, raised designs.)

2. Arrange the inked leaves on a piece of stationery as you would like them to print.

3. Position an envelope face down over the leaves on the stationery as you would like it to be printed, and press with the heel of your hand. Inking the stationery and the envelope at the same time will allow you to design a matched set.

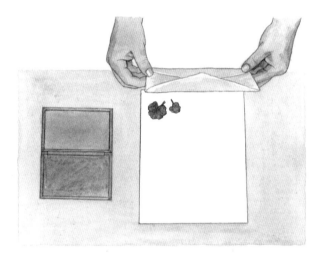

4. Remove envelope and leaf carefully and allow printed paper to dry before packaging as a gift.

Variation: To create two prints at once, simply place a second sheet of stationery facedown over leaves in Step 2.

HAMMERED PRINT T-SHIRT

adapted from *Nature Printing with Herbs, Fruits & Flowers*

This printing technique requires no paint or ink. Naturally occurring pigments, such as green chlorophyll, are released when a young, juicy leaf is pummeled on natural fiber fabric. The resulting pigmented design is then set in a mineral bath.

Hammered-leaf and fabric-paint nature prints can be combined on a T-shirt.

What You Will Need

Fresh, young leaves
**Natural fiber T-shirt or fabric,
   prewashed and ironed**
Hammer with a flat end
Newspapers
Waxed paper
Transparent tape
Salt or washing soda
Wood ashes (optional)
Water
Iron

1. Lay a section of newspaper topped with a sheet of waxed paper on a hard, flat surface.

2. Spread the T-shirt or fabric on the surface so that the area to be printed on is smoothed with no wrinkles and then arrange the leaves you intend to print. Secure all edges of each leaf to the fabric with tape (see figure 1). Cover leaves with another sheet of waxed paper.

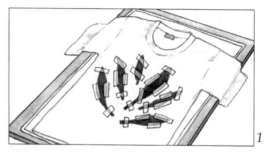

3. Hammer leaves for several minutes until prints appear (see figure 2). Replace the waxed paper cover as needed, if it rips. Some leaves may print better than others, and coloration will vary. Very fragile leaves disintegrate quickly. You may want to experiment first on a piece of scrap fabric, and then select the leaves that work best.

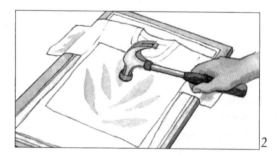

4. To set colorfastness, soak the T-shirt or fabric in a solution of ½ cup salt to 2 gallons tepid water for ten minutes, or in a solution of 2 tablespoons washing soda dissolved in 2 gallons tepid water for ten minutes. Rinse thoroughly and dry outdoors or in a dryer. Iron fabric smooth.

5. Then gift wrap your finished project in some of your favorite hand-printed or store-purchased paper. Or simply roll up the T-shirt or fabric neatly and tie it with a beautiful satin ribbon.

Variation: For a reddish-brown color, follow directions in step 4 for a mineral bath and rinse, then immediately soak in 3 gallons of cold water mixed with 1 cup of wood ashes for five minutes. Rinse again, dry, and iron.

Gifts for the Bath

Bath salts, oils, and herbal baths are easy to make and always warmly welcomed, perfect for a friend or loved one who has a stressful lifestyle and enjoys unwinding with a long, luxurious bath. Bathing has of course been an important daily ritual for thousands of years, pampering the body and the spirit. Cleopatra was known for her soothing milk baths and Marie Antoinette for her long, luxurious herbal ones. Gifts for the bath carry on this timeless tradition in a time-bound world.

Whether you are purchasing or packaging essential oils, you should ensure that they are kept in full, dark glass bottles. Plastic bottles are porous and will allow the essential oil to dissipate. Dark-colored glass, such as blue, green, or brown, is necessary to protect essential oils from light, which will diminish their potency. Essential oils should also be kept in full bottles, as contact with air will accelerate their deterioration. If you are packaging your own oils, whether for yourself or as a gift, you can often find decorative, dark glass bottles in antique stores, at flea markets, or at bath and gift shops. Make sure the lids fit tightly.

BATH OILS

adapted from *The Essential Oils Book*

Bath oils are a great treat for a spouse or special friend — especially at holiday time. An age-old treatment for dry skin, scented oils can also be mentally relaxing, stimulating, and sensual.

Adding Essential Oils to Your Bath

Essential oils should be added to the bath just before you enter the tub. If added to the water while the tub is filling, much of the oils' precious essences goes up in steam and very little is left to be absorbed by the skin. Once you've added the oils, be sure to mix them into the water well. It is very important to avoid direct skin contact with undiluted essential oils that may irritate or cause skin sensitivity. You can also dilute the essential oils in a carrier oil before adding them to the bath, or, as some people prefer, in ¼ cup milk or cream.

WAKE UP BATH I

This is a refreshing blend that leaves you feeling awake and energized.

3   **drops rosemary**
3   **drops lemon**
2   **drops eucalyptus**

For bath: Oils should be added directly to a tub full of warm water and mixed well.

For shampoo or shower soap: Add blend to 1 ounce unscented shampoo or liquid castile soap.

For massage or hair oil: Add blend to 1 ounce base oil.

WAKE UP BATH II

Here is a slight variation of the above recipe.

3   **drops rosemary**
2   **drops peppermint**
3   **drops lemon**

Follow the same directions as for *Wake Up Bath I.*

RELAXING BATH

This blend smells wonderful and will help you to unwind after a long day.

5   **drops lavender**
2   **drops ylang-ylang**
2   **drops rose absolute or otto (also called attar)**

For bath: Oils should be added directly to a tub full of warm bath water and mixed well.

For massage: Add to ½ ounce base oil and 2 drops Roman chamomile (optional) and massage over the body before rest.

COLD CARE BATH

This pungent blend opens the nose, soothes aching muscles, and relieves congestion.

6   **drops eucalyptus**
3   **drops frankincense**
3   **drops hyssop**
2   **drops ylang-ylang, rose geranium, or jasmine absolute (optional)**

For bath: Add oils directly to a tub full of warm water and mix well.

As inhalant: Add blend to a simmer pot in a sick room. Be sure to watch the water level.

For massage oil: Add blend to ½ ounce base oil and massage into chest, arms, neck, and abdomen. (Before using, test for skin sensitivity first by applying to a small patch of skin on the inside of your arm.)

For treatment on the go: If you must go to work while suffering from a cold, try blending these oils and adding them to tissues.

Store them in a bag you can carry all day and inhale as often as possible.

ANTIDEPRESSANT BATH

This is a relaxing, soothing blend that relieves heaviness in heart and mind.

3   **drops bergamot**
3   **drops rosewood**
3   **drops lavender**
2   **drops rose otto**

For bath: Add oils directly to a tub full of warm water and mix well.

For massage: Add essential oils to ½ ounce base oil and massage over the entire body, especially the heart area. For a full-body massage, double the amounts in recipe.

Bath-Oil Gift Bottles

Make up bath-oil blends in larger quantities to divide up and package as gifts in dark glass bottles. You can use either pure, undiluted essential oils or a blend of oils diluted in a base oil to use as a skin softener. For undiluted bath blends, you'll need bottles that hold ½ to 1 ounce; for diluted floating bath blends, purchase 2- to 4-ounce sizes.

Make the gift complete by creating a nice label that clearly states the ingredients, cautions, and directions for adding oils to the bath, and number of drops to use (or capfuls in the case of diluted blends). I always include the date the blend was made and my initials as well. If you are making a large quantity of bath blend for several gifts, you can order decorative address labels by mail with your blend information printed in place of your name and address.

I like to make labels from either ready-made sticky-backs or paper cards that can be hung from the bottle neck. If you use sticky-back labels, cover them with a protective layer of clear tape once they're on the bottle so they last longer. Paper cards can be hole punched and tied on the bottle with a piece of ribbon. Tie on a glass eyedropper with each bottle, unless you can find bottles with dropper inserts. Eyedroppers come in sizes to fit specific bottles. I use ones that fit 4 ml (1 dram) and 15 ml (approximately ½ ounce) amber bottles.

OTHER BATH-OIL COMBINATIONS

Here are some other possible combinations of essential oils that make good bath blends. You can mix and match the amounts of each ingredient depending on your personal preference.

- lavender, ylang-ylang, patchouli, and rose absolute
- lemon, juniper, grapefruit, and rosemary
- bergamot, rosewood, sandalwood, frankincense, and clary sage
- lavender, rose geranium, and patchouli
- sweet orange, vanilla oleoresin, and frankincense

BATH SALTS

adapted from *The Essential Oils Book*

Bath salts make great stocking-stuffers or Hannukah gifts. There are endless combinations of essential oils for bath salts. These are a few favorites that work well. The recipes can be easily doubled to make more.

Make sure the salt is well dissolved in the bath water or you will end up sitting on uncomfortable little lumps. Remember to keep the container of bath salts tightly sealed to prevent the volatile essential oils and absolutes from escaping into the environment and reducing the potency and effects of the bath salts.

BATH SALTS COMBINATION #1

This is a balancing, refreshing blend. If desired, add 1 or 2 drops of a citrus oil like lemon, sweet orange, or tangerine to brighten this blend.

- 3 **drops rosewood**
- 3 **drops bergamot**
- 2 **drops frankincense**
- 2 **cups (500 ml) sea salt**

Bath-Salts Gift Jars

When properly sealed, bath salts can last a long time. To ensure a longer shelf life, do not add base oil to the salt (you can include instructions for doing this just before use on the label). Find a pretty jar or decorative tin, and give this gift to a friend who's experiencing exasperating times. (You might want to put a small muslin bag of rice in the bottom of the container of salt to absorb any moisture that might find its way into the container.)

Wrap the container in some pretty paper you've purchased or printed and gather at the top with ribbon or twine. Attach a hand-printed card detailing instructions for use.

BATH SALTS COMBINATION #2

These essential oils are known to help cleanse toxins from the body, and the scent is clean and fresh. Drinking a lot of water is also very important when cleansing the body of any impurities, as is maintaining a healthy diet and lifestyle.

3   drops lavender
3   drops grapefruit
2   drops juniper
2   cups (500 ml) sea salt

For a "skinny bath": Make sure the oils are well mixed with the salt to avoid skin irritation from these salts, which have been found to help relieve cellulite. The bath should be followed up with an application of the oils blended in ½ ounce base oil to problem areas. Cypress oil is a good addition.

BATH SALTS COMBINATION #3

This is an earthy, grounding blend that men especially like.

3   drops sandalwood
3   drops patchouli
3   drops lavender
2   cups (500 ml) sea salt

Caution

Some essential oils, including bergamot and citrus oils such as lemon and orange, may increase the skin's sensitivity to the sun. The citrus oils can also increase the skin pigmentation in some people. If not properly blended and applied unevenly, darkening and skin irritation could result. Avoid sun exposure for six hours following use.

Herb Bath Balls

Herbs can quiet the nerves and temper emotions, transforming tension into calmness and anxiety into pleasure. Make herbal bath balls to use as a stocking stuffers, or incorporate them into your packaging for larger gifts.

RELAXING HERB BATH BAGS

adapted from *The Essential Oils Book*

Surprise a special friend or spouse with this fragrant herbal confection, just made for dropping into a warm bath prior to a long soak.

What You Will Need
Printed fabric cut in 4-inch squares
Mixture of 4–5 bath herbs*
Wool yarn cut into 10-inch lengths

* Suitable bath herbs include: calendula, chamomile, comfrey, garden sage, lavender, lemongrass, peppermint, rosemary, rose, spearmint, thyme, and yarrow.

1. Cut fabric into 4-inch squares. Place 1 teaspoon of herb mixture in the center of each fabric square.
2. Draw up the four corners, and tie tightly into a sachet using the yarn lengths.
3. Each ball makes one relaxing bath. Toss it into a warm bath like a large tea bag and squeeze often to release the oils from the herbs.

Holiday Stress Reduction

To make your own holiday season more calm, collect ingredients in advance. (They are readily available either from your garden, your pantry shelves, or your nearest herb shop.) Combine the mixture well ahead of the holidays, storing it in a clear glass jar, and you'll be ready to create a dozen or more bath balls on a moment's notice.

When you're ready to present these delightful gifts, add a personalized instruction tag such as, "For a most relaxing herbal bath, drop entire bath ball into a warm (not hot) bath and enjoy yourself as the fragrance envelops you."

AROMATIC BATH BASKET

adapted from *The Essential Oils Book*

This basket of aromatic allies will be a cherished gift. Mix and match as you see fit to create a custom-made aromatic bath basket for each person on your holiday gift list.

Things to Include

Two herbal bath bags (see page 21)
A jar of bath salts (see page 19)
A loofah or scrub
An assortment of essential oils in 4 ml bottles with eye-droppers, with directions for blending and using*
A small bottle of sweet almond base oil (2–4 ounces)

*Some appropriate essential oils would be: lavender, rosemary, sandalwood, ylang-ylang, rose geranium, grapefruit, clary sage, bergamot, or rosewood.

Line a basket with a fine washcloth or small towel and sprinkle a mixture of dried herbs in the bottom before adding the assortment of gifts. Use herbs you've included in the bath bags, or lavender and rose buds for beauty, calendula petals for brightness, or mint leaves for an aromatic and stimulating tone. Be sure to label each item and add directions for using.

Facial Tonics

adapted from *Herbal Vinegar*

Cosmetic vinegars — also called toilet vinegars — have been an indispensable complexion aid for centuries, and they make thoughtful gifts today. Able to close pores and preserve or restore the skin's natural acidity, or proper pH balance, vinegars keep both oily and dry complexions soft and fresh. Vinegar tonics are much better for the skin than most commercial tonics because the latter usually contain drying alcohol. Vinegar tonics also combat the ravages of alkaline soaps and makeup. Depending on the herbs infused in the vinegar, tonics can tone, heal, soothe, or soften the skin of both women and men. They can also keep acne at bay, improve circulation, reduce broken veins and capillaries, smooth out wrinkles, and bleach freckles.

To create a vinegar facial tonic, dilute it with six parts of spring water, rose water, or orange flower water, to be splashed on the face after washing, or applied with a cotton ball. For cosmetic use, choose a high-quality apple cider vinegar or an herb-infused cider or wine vinegar, prepared as any culinary herb vinegar.

Herbal Vinegars through the Ages

Through the ages, many different "recipes" for cosmetic herbal vinegars have evolved. Floral vinegars, such as lavender, jasmine, rose, and pinks, have been especially favored for tonics, but many of the more traditional culinary herbs have been recognized as good for the skin as well. Cosmetic vinegars can be as strong or as delicate as you like. A good proportion to start with is 1 cup of fresh petals or leaves for each 2 cups of vinegar, steeped for several weeks and then strained and bottled.

BASIC COSMETIC VINEGAR I

(for the bath, face, or hair)

2   ounces fresh (or 1 ounce dried) each of: thyme leaves, lavender flowers, spearmint leaves, rosemary leaves, and sage leaves

4   cups apple cider or wine vinegar

¼   ounce gum camphor

½   ounce gum benzoin

3   tablespoons grain alcohol

1. Mix together the fresh or dried herbs.

2. Steep mixture with the vinegar for several weeks, then strain.

3. Mix together gum camphor, gum benzoin, and alcohol until dissolved. Stir into vinegar, cover, and let stand for three days.

4. Strain, bottle, cap tightly, and label.

BASIC COSMETIC VINEGAR II

(for the bath, skin, or hair)

2   ounces fresh (or 1 ounce dried) each of: dried orange peel, leaves, and flowers; rose leaves, petals, and hips; willow bark; and chamomile flowers

4   cups apple cider or wine vinegar

1   cup rose water

1. Mix together the fresh or dried ingredients.

2. Steep with vinegar for several weeks, then strain. Add rose water. Bottle, cap tightly, and label.

HERBAL VINEGAR FACIAL TONIC COMBINATIONS

Apple Cider Vinegar or Wine Vinegar

Orange peel, orange mint leaves, and calendula petals
Lavender flowers, lady's mantle leaves, and rose petals
Rose petals, chamomile flowers, and rose water
Lavender flowers and rosemary, mint, and thyme leaves
Lavender flowers and mint leaves
Calendula petals and witch hazel

Therapeutic Herbs and Their Properties

A number of herbs have been shown to contribute to general good health. You might consider using some of the following steeped in vinegar for the reason given.

Acacia/*Acacia* spp. Astringent, soothes and heals dry skin.

Bay/*Laurus nobilis.* Antiseptic, stimulates.

Calendula/*Calendula officinalis.* Astringent, soothes, softens, heals, clears blemishes.

Chamomile/*Chamaemelum nobile.* For normal skin, antiseptic, astringent, cleanses, softens, soothes.

Colts foot/*Tussilago farfara.* Stimulates circulation, heals sores.

Comfrey/*Symphytum offincinale.* Heals, soothes, for burns and swellings, astringent.

Echinacea/*Echinacea angustifolia.* Antiseptic, heals, improves circulation.

Elderflowers/*Sambucus* spp. For dry skin, softens, heals, cleanses, whitens skin.

Fennel/*Foeniculum vulgare.* Cleanses, invigorates, astringent, smooths.

Honeysuckle/*Lonicera* spp. Antiseptic, astringent.

Juniper/*Juniperus communis.* Relieves sore muscles/joints, antiseptic, stimulates.

Lavender/*Lavandula angustifolia.* Treatment for oily skin, stimulates, antiseptic, relieves joint pain.

Lemon balm/*Melissa officinalis.* Soothes, astringent, cleanses, smooths.

Lemon peel/*Citrus limon.* Treatment for oily skin, stimulates, astringent, tonic.

Lovage/*Levistichum officinale.* Cleanses, deodorizes.

Marjoram/*Origanum majorana.* Antiseptic, heals, soothes, relieves aching muscles and joints.

Mint/*Mentha* spp. For normal skin, refreshes, cools, heals, stimulates, astringent, relieves headaches.

Orange/*Citrus* spp. Treatment for dry skin, soothes.

Oregano/*Origanum vulgare.* Antiseptic, heals, soothes, relieves aching muscles and joints.

Parsley/*Petroselinum crispum.* For oily skin, cleanses, lightens freckles, adds shine to dark hair.

Rose/*Rosa* spp. For normal skin, astringent, hydrates, heals, soothes.

Rosemary/*Rosmarinus officinalis.* For oily skin, stimulates, antiseptic, insect repellent, soothes, heals.

Rue/*Ruta graveolens.* Stimulates, heals, soothes, relieves muscle and joint pain.

Sage/*Salvia officinalis.* For oily skin, stimulates, strong astringent, relieves aching muscles.

Thyme/*Thymus* spp. Antiseptic, stimulates, deodorizes.

Violet/*Viola* spp. Clears blemishes, stimulates, heals, soothes.

Willow/*Salix alba.* Disinfectant, astringent, relieves muscle and joint pain and fevers and chills.

Yarrow/*Achillea millefolium.* For oily skin, astringent, cleanses, heals, improves circulation, relieves joint and muscle pain, reduces fever.

Holiday Ornaments

Handcrafted ornaments made from natural objects are wonderful and unique gifts. Each ornament lends an enduring festive element to its surroundings and can carry the holiday spirit on through the rest of the year. Best of all, these ornaments are easy and inexpensive to make. Make the natural world an integral part of your holiday celebrations with these fragrant and lovely ornaments.

APPLE CONE TREE

adapted from *Herbal Treasures*

These are delightful and aromatic gifts. You can change the color of the ribbon or the apples to make a decorated cone for any holiday occasion. If your dried apple slices have not been treated with a sealer, keep the apple cone tree away from areas of high humidity.

What You Will Need
1 large (6 to 8 inches tall) pine cone
Dried apple slices (approximately 1½ cups)
Small sprays of baby's breath
3 or more 6-inch lengths of ⅛-inch ribbon
Glue gun and glue sticks

1. Level the bottom of the pine cone by rocking it back and forth on a flat, solid surface to break off uneven petals from the bottom.

2. Cut a large, dried apple slice in half and fold to form a cone shape. Glue the ends together and allow to dry. This will form the base of the apple cone tree. Apply hot glue to the tip of the cone-shaped apple slice and place the pine cone over the tip. Allow to dry.

3. Starting at the top of the pine cone and using the smallest apple slices first, insert the apple slices between the cone petals, skin side out, to test for fit before gluing. To glue, run a small bead of hot glue along the edge of the apple slice and insert the slice between the cone petals.

4. Glue small sprays of baby's breath scattered around the cone. Tie 6-inch lengths of ribbon into small bows and glue them on the edges of the cone petals. You can also tie ribbon onto small pieces of cinnamon sticks, and glue the sticks onto the cone.

Variation: You can scent the cone by adding a few drops of essential oil along the edges of the cone petals.

POTPOURRI POMANDER

adapted from *Herbal Treasures*

This decoration, with its sweet, old-fashioned look, makes a delightful gift. You can use an apple or orange for your base if you prefer, although the Styrofoam ball tends to last longer.

What You Will Need

Crochet yarn or fine wire (of a length sufficient to hang the pomander
3-inch Styrofoam ball
Clove or toothpick
Oakmoss
Glue
Velvet ribbon for a bow
An assortment of flowers and spice, such as allspice, balm-of-Gilead buds, 1-inch cinnamon sticks, tiny heather flowers, whole rose hips, sandalwood chips, sunflower petals, or others (see Assortment A and Assortment B on page 29)

---

1. Thread the crochet yarn through a long darning needle, knot the two ends together, and push the needle through the center of the Styrofoam ball. Push a clove or a 1-inch piece of toothpick through the knot at the end of the yarn, and pull this end tight against the ball to prevent the yarn from pulling through. If you are using wire, double it and force the center folded point through the ball. Fold back 1 inch of wire on each of the two loose ends and tuck these up into the ball securely to keep the wire in place.

2. Place the oakmoss on a sheet of newspaper. Coat the ball in glue and roll it in the oakmoss until it is completely covered. Allow to dry.

3. Arrange the flowers and spices over the oakmoss, using plenty of glue.

4. Make a bow out of the velvet ribbon, using multiple loops and long streamers if desired. Attach the bow to the top or bottom of the pomander.

Variation: Add a few drops of essential oil in several places over the surface. The oakmoss will act as a fixative. Refresh with oil from time to time.

Combinations for Your Pomander

Assortment A	Assortment B
Rosebuds and petals (pink)	Hibiscus flowers (maroon)
Star anise (brown)	Calcitrippae flowers (deep blue)
Cloves (brown)	Statice flowers (pink/purple)
French lavender (purple)	Roman chamomile (cream)
Everlastings (yellow)	White cardamom seeds (cream)
Malva flowers (black)	Uva-ursi leaves (green)

MINIATURE TUSSIE MUSSIES

adapted from *Herbal Treasures*

*Miniature tussie mussies make elegant holiday ornaments and are a
perfect way to use pieces of herbs and flowers left over from wreaths.*

What You Will Need

Styrofoam
8-inch lengths of fine wire
Very small sprigs and pieces of flowers, herbs, and spices
Glue
Narrow width of lace
Sturdy white paper
Florists tape
Short length of ¼-inch wide ribbon

1. Cut a piece of Styrofoam about the size of a nickel.
   Double a length of wire and push the folded center
   point through the center of the Styrofoam circle to
   make a handle. Leave about an inch of the loose
   ends protruding from the bottom (see figure 1).
   Thread the cord under the wireloop on top of the
   styrofoam, and tie it off to make a loop handle.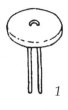

2. Push the stems of the herbs into the Styrofoam. If you have
   one, use a single, tiny rosebud in the center. Use glue to affix
   any herb, spice, or flower that doesn't have a sturdy stem. Use
   single florets of rosebuds, statice, tansy, or other flower to make
   a tiny bouquet on the Styrofoam, filling in the spaces with tiny
   whole cloves, tiny sprigs of baby's breath, leaves
   of boxwood, or other tiny blossoms. Allow to dry.

3. Wrap the lace around the base of the tussie
   mussie, cut to fit, and glue around the edge. Cover
   the bottom with a fitted circle of white paper, first
   snipping off any stem ends that may protrude.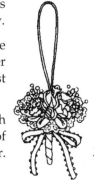

4. Wrap together the two loose ends of the wire with
   florist's tape. Then finish off with a tiny bow of
   ribbon in a matching or complementary color.
   (See figure 2).

PRESSED HERB ORNAMENT

adapted from *Herbal Treasures*

As herbs bloom, save the tiny blossoms and a few leaves. Press and dry these snippets to use in this wonderfully elegant and delicate holiday ornament.

What You Will Need

Pressed and dried small cuttings from herb plants
    (good choices are thyme, sage, lavender, marjoram,
    rue, hyssop, the individual florets of chive and bee
    balm, and the smaller leaves of bay and costmary)
2 microscope slides
Transparent glue
Sewing needle or pin
⅛-inch wide satin or grosgrain ribbon

---

1. Arrange the cuttings of herbs on a microscope slide. Secure carefully with tiny drops of glue applied with the point of a needle or pin. Allow to dry.

2. Cover the arrangement with the other microscope slide. Secure at the corners with additional glue droplets. Press until dry.

3. Make a 1-inch loop of the ribbon and glue it to the center of the top edge. When the loop is dry, make a border with the rest of the ribbon, covering the raw edges of the glass. Beginning at the top center, glue the ribbon in place all the way around, ending at the center and leaving 4–5 inches of ribbon at each end. Allow to dry.

4. Tie the ends of the ribbon in a bow around the hanging loop. Trim the ends to an attractive length.

Other Storey Titles You Will Enjoy

***Drawn to Nature Through the Journals
of Clare Walker Leslie.***
An invitation to readers to take a moment to slow
down and see nature with renewed appreciation.
176 pages. Paper with flaps. ISBN 978-1-58017-614-9.

Keeping a Nature Journal,
by Clare Walker Leslie & Charles E. Roth.
Simple methods for capturing the living
beauty of each season.
224 pages. Paper with flaps. ISBN 978-1-58017-493-0.

Making Herbal Dream Pillows, by Jim Long.
Step-by-step instructions and lavish, full-color illustrations
that show how to create herbal dream blends and pillows.
64 pages. Hardcover with jacket. ISBN 978-1-58017-075-8.

Nature's Art Box, by Laura C. Martin.
Cool projects for crafty kids to make
with natural materials.
224 pages. Paper. ISBN 978-1-58017-490-9.

Organic Body Care Recipes,
by Stephanie Tourles.
Homemade, herbal formulas for glowing
skin, hair, and nails, plus a vibrant self.
384 pages. Paper. ISBN 978-1-58017-676-7.

***Rosemary Gladstar's Herbal Recipes
for Vibrant Health.***
A practical compendium of herbal lore and know-how
for wellness, longevity, and boundless energy.
408 pages. Paper. ISBN 978-1-60342-078-5.

These and other books from Storey Publishing are available
wherever quality books are sold or by calling 1-800-441-5700.
Visit us at *www.storey.com* or sign up for our newsletter
at *www.storey.com/signup.*